Little Women

LOUISA M. ALCOTT

Level 1

Retold by M. Albers
Series Editors: Andy Hopkins and Jocelyn Potter

Pearson Education Limited
Edinburgh Gate, Harlow,
Essex CM20 2JE, England
and Associated Companies throughout the world.

ISBN 0 582 41668 X

First published 1868
First published by Puffin Books 1953
This edition first published 2000

7 9 10 8

Typeset by Digital Type, London
Set in 12/14pt Bembo
Printed in Spain by Mateu Cromo, S. A. Pinto (Madrid)

Published by Pearson Education Limited in association with
Penguin Books Ltd, both companies being subsidiaries of Pearson Plc

For a complete list of titles available in the Penguin Readers series please write to your local
Pearson Education office or contact: Penguin Readers Marketing Department,
Pearson Education, Edinburgh Gate, Harlow, Essex, CM20 2JE.

Introduction

It was six in the evening and the girls were at home. They talked about Christmas.

Jo wasn't happy.

"It's Christmas and we aren't going to have any presents!" she said.

Jo March and her three sisters don't have any money for Christmas presents. They can't buy presents, and they aren't going to get presents from their family. Their father is away, and their mother wants to give their food to a family with seven children. Is the March family going to have a very unhappy Christmas?

Little Women is about the four girls. They have happy times, but they have problems too. Can Jo go to a party with a burn in her dress? Who is the Laurence boy? And where is Meg's glove? This is a story of family love in difficult times.

Louisa May Alcott (1832–88) came from Pennsylvania, in the United States. Her father was a teacher, and she had three sisters. They didn't have much money, and the children worked.

Louisa liked writing stories. The problems of the Marches in *Little Women* (1868) were problems in Louisa's family too. Jo's story is Louisa's story.

There are four books about the March family. After *Little Women* came *Little Men*, *Good Wives*, and *Jo's Boys*.

Chapter 1   A Letter From Father

It was two days before Christmas.

Meg, Jo, Beth, and Amy March were sisters. Meg was sixteen and she was very beautiful. She had big eyes and beautiful long brown hair. Jo was fifteen. She was tall and thin. She had dark eyes and long brown hair. Beth was thirteen. She was very quiet. Little Amy had blue eyes and yellow hair.

It was six in the evening and the girls were at home. They talked about Christmas.

Jo wasn't happy.

"It's Christmas and we aren't going to have any presents!" she said.

Meg looked at her old dress.

"I know, Jo," she said. "But we don't have much money."

Amy said, "My friends are going to have presents. I want some presents too."

Beth smiled.

"We don't have any money," she said. "But we have Mother and Father, and we're happy."

Jo didn't smile.

She said, "We don't have Father. He's away in the war and he isn't coming back for Christmas."

"Maybe he isn't going to come back," the girls thought. But they didn't say it.

"We have a little money," Meg said. "What can we buy?"

"I want a new book," Jo said. She loved reading.

"And I'd like some pens," Amy said.

"I don't want any presents," Beth said. "Let's buy presents for Mother. We can put them on the table for her on Christmas Day."

"Yes," said Jo. "Let's do that. We can buy them tomorrow. What can we get for her?"

Then Mrs. March arrived in her dark coat and old hat. She called, "Children, I'm home!"

"Hello, Mother!" the girls answered.

"Come and kiss me, girls!" Mrs. March said. They went to her, and she smiled at them. "I have a letter from Father," she said. "Let's eat, and then we can read it."

Later in the evening, Mrs. March said, "Sit down now, girls. I'm going to read Father's letter to you."

It was a happy letter. Father didn't talk about the war. The letter finished:

Give my love and a kiss to my little women. A year is a long time, but I think of them every day.

The girls were very unhappy. They wanted their father. They thought about his letter.

"I'm going to be good this year," Amy said.

"I don't like my work," Meg said, "but I'm going to do it well."

"I want to be a 'little woman' for Father," Jo said. "I'm often angry, but I'm going to stop now."

Beth didn't talk. She looked at the floor.

"Don't be unhappy, girls!" Mrs. March said. "Let's play a game."

After the game, Beth played the old piano. Then Mrs. March said, "Good night, girls. Sleep well!"

It was a happy letter. Father didn't talk about the war.

She kissed her daughters, and the four girls went up to bed.

Chapter 2   Christmas Day

On Christmas morning, Meg, Jo, Beth, and Amy opened their eyes and looked under their beds. There were four books there. Meg's book was green, Jo's was red, Beth's was white, and Amy's was blue.

"Oh, Mother!" they thought. "You *are* good to us."

Hannah lived in the house and she helped Mrs. March.

Meg opened her book and started to read it. Her sisters listened.

Later, they went down to the kitchen. Hannah was there. She lived in the house and she helped Mrs. March. There was food on the table.

"Where's Mother?" Meg asked.

"I don't know," Hannah answered. "She went out very early."

Amy looked out the window.

"She's coming down the street!" she said.

"Quickly!" Jo said. "Put her presents away!"

Mrs. March came into the house.

"Good morning, Mother!" the girls called.

"Where were you?" Jo asked.

Mrs March answered, "I went to Mrs. Hummel's house. She has seven small children. They don't have any food and they're very cold." She looked at her daughters. Then she said, "It's Christmas, girls. Can we give them our food?"

The girls looked at the food. They wanted to eat, but they said quickly, "Oh, yes, Mother. Can *we* take it?"

They went to the Hummels with a big bag of food.

Later in the morning, the girls said, "Here are your presents, Mother!"

"Oh! Thank you. You're good children," Mrs. March said. She looked at her presents and smiled.

◆

They went to the Hummels.

They loved acting and their friends had a good time.

In the evening, the girls' friends came, and the girls acted for them. They loved acting and their friends had a good time.

Then Hannah said, "Come and eat, children!"

On the table there was a lot of food and some fruit and candy. The girls looked at it with open eyes. Where did it come from?

"It's from Santa Claus!"★ Beth said.

"No, Mother did it," Meg said.

Jo said, "It's from Aunt March! Maybe she likes us on Christmas Day. She doesn't usually like us."

★ In some countries, children hear a story about Santa Claus at Christmas. In the story, Santa Claus brings presents for children on the night before Christmas.

"You're wrong," Mrs. March said. "It's from old Mr. Laurence. You see him sometimes—he lives near here."

"Yes, but we don't *know* him!" Meg said.

"He was a friend of my father," Mrs. March said. "He knows about the food for the Hummels. This food is for you from him because you didn't eat well this morning."

Jo's friend said, "My mother knows old Mr. Laurence. He's a good man, but he doesn't see many people. His daughter's dead and her son lives with him. The boy's name's Laurie."

"I want to meet Laurie," Jo said. "We don't know many boys. Maybe he can act."

"He can visit us," Mrs. March said.

Jo smiled.

"Oh," Beth said to her mother, "*we're* very happy. But Father isn't happy."

"No," Mrs. March said quietly. She kissed her daughter.

"I want to see him," Beth said. "I want to give him a present."

"I know, Beth. I know."

Chapter 3   The Party

Five days later, Meg came quickly into the house.

"Jo! Jo!" she called. "Where are you?"

"Here," Jo called. "I'm reading."

Meg had a letter in her hand. "Listen. This letter's from Mrs. Gardiner. It's for you and me, and it says,

'Please come to a small party tomorrow evening.' I talked to Mother, and we can go."

"Oh!" said Jo. "A New Year's party!"

"Yes," Meg said. "But we don't have the right dresses."

Jo said, "And I have a burn on my good dress."

"You can sit on a chair all evening," Meg said. "Then people can't see the burn. Don't dance!"

Before the party, Beth and Amy helped Meg and Jo with their dresses and their hair.

"I can curl your hair with some hot curlers, Meg," Jo said to her sister.

Suddenly, Beth said. "Oh, look—Meg's hair! It's burning!"

"Oh! Oh! Oh!" Meg said. "My hair! My hair! I can't go to the party now!"

"Meg's hair! It's burning!"

But Amy said, "Put a ribbon in your hair. There—you can't see the burn now."

Beth kissed Meg and said, "You're beautiful."

"Do you have your gloves, girls?" Mrs. March asked. "Good. Have a good time, and come home at eleven."

◆

At the party, the music played and Meg danced.

A tall boy with red hair walked across the room to Jo.

"Can we dance?" he asked her.

Jo wanted to dance, but she thought about the burn on her dress. She smiled and said "no."

Then she went quickly into a small, quiet room. But the Laurence boy was there.

"Oh! I *am* sorry," Jo said. "I didn't see you." She looked at him. "You live in the big house near our house. My name's Josephine March, but people call me Jo."

The boy smiled. "Hello. I'm Laurie," he said.

"Laurie Laurence?" Jo asked.

"My name's Theodore," he said. "But I don't like it because boys called me 'Dora.' Now I'm Laurie."

"We loved your Christmas present," Jo said. "Do you like parties?"

"Sometimes. I was in France for years, and I don't know people here."

"France!" Jo said. "Can you talk French?"

Jo and Laurie talked and talked. Laurie liked music.

"Listen to the piano!" Jo said. "Let's go and dance."

"Yes, let's do that," Laurie said.

"Oh!" Jo said suddenly. "I can't—"

"Why?" Laurie asked.

"I have a burn in the back of my dress. I can't dance."

Laurie smiled. "People aren't going to look," he said. "Please come."

◆

The party finished and Jo and Meg went home. They went up to their bedroom. Amy and Beth were in bed, but they quickly opened their eyes.

Amy said, "Did you have a good time?"

"Oh yes," Meg said.

"And you, Jo?" Beth asked.

"Yes, I had a good time too," Jo said. "Here's some candy from the party."

They talked for a long time about the party and about Laurie.

Chapter 4   The Laurences

One cold morning, Meg and Jo didn't want to get up.

"I don't want to work today," Meg said.

"I want to stay at home too," Jo said, "but we can't do that."

Meg was the teacher for four children in the King family. The job was difficult, because the children only wanted to play.

Jo worked at Aunt March's house. Aunt March was Father's sister, but she had a lot of money. Jo liked her house because she had a lot of books. But Aunt March was an angry woman, and Jo didn't always like her.

Amy went to school every day. Beth was a very quiet girl and she didn't want to go to school. She helped Hannah in the house and she had a teacher at home.

◆

In the afternoon, Jo came home from Aunt March's house. She looked up at the Laurences' big house. Laurie was at a window.

Jo called, "Hello. How are you? Are you sick?"

Laurie answered, "No, I *was* sick, but now I'm well again. Come and talk to me."

Jo went into Laurie's house and they talked.

Jo thought, "Laurie doesn't see many people—only old Mr. Laurence and his teacher, Mr. Brooke."

"What are you thinking, Miss Jo?" Laurie said.

She answered, "Come and visit us. You can meet Mother and my sisters. Beth can play the piano and Amy can dance for you. Meg and I can talk to you."

Laurie smiled. "I'd like that," he said.

There was a noise at the door. Then Laurie said, "Excuse me, the doctor's here. Can you wait?"

"Yes, of course," Jo said.

In the room there was a picture of Mr. Laurence. Jo looked at it and said, "His face isn't very friendly, but I like him."

"Thank you," said a man behind her.

It was old Mr. Laurence! Jo's face was very red, but the old man smiled.

"How do you do?" he said. "Come and sit with me."

Laurie came back, and Jo talked about her family with him and Mr. Laurence.

After this visit, the March girls often played at Laurie's house and he came to their home. Beth often played the piano there. It was a good piano, and Mr. Laurence liked listening to her music.

"I had a little girl with your eyes," he said to her one day. "She played the piano too. She was Laurie's mother."

Then one day there was a piano in the March family's front yard. The letter on it said, "To Miss Elizabeth March."

"For me!" Beth said.

"Yes, it's a present for you from Mr. Laurence," Jo said.

Quiet little Beth went quickly to the big house.

After this visit, the March girls often played at Laurie's house.

"Thank you! Thank you!" she said to the old man.

Then she kissed him.

After that, the Marches and the Laurences were very good friends.

Chapter 5   Problems for Amy

"I want some money," Amy said one day. "It's important."

"Why, Amy?" Meg asked.

"Every day my friends take candy to school. I eat their candy, but I can't buy it for *them*."

"Here's a little money for you," Meg said. "But please don't ask again. We don't have a lot of money, you know."

"Oh, thank you, Meg," Amy said.

In the morning, at school, Amy had the candy in her bag. Now every girl wanted to be Amy's friend.

Katy Brown said, "Please come to my party."

Then Jenny Snow said, "Can I have some candy? I can help you with your schoolwork."

"No, you can't have any candy," Amy said. "Yesterday you said, 'Amy March is fat!' "

She walked away.

Jenny Snow was angry, and she went to the teacher.

"Mr. Davis," she said. "Amy March has some candy in her school bag."

Mr. Davis was angry too. He didn't like candy at school.

"Amy March," he said. "Come here. Bring me your candy."

Amy walked to Mr. Davis's table at the front of the room.

He said, "Never bring candy to school again! Do you hear me?"

"Yes, Mr. Davis," Amy said.

Then he said, "Your hand, Miss March."

Amy closed her eyes, and Mr. Davis hit her hand.

"Now stand here at my table," he said. "Don't move."

Amy's face was red and she was very unhappy.

Later, the teacher said, "You can sit down now, Miss March."

But Amy didn't sit down. She didn't talk to Mr. Davis or the girls. She was angry and unhappy. She went home.

"Amy, what's wrong?" Mrs. March asked. "Why are you home from school early?"

Amy said, "Mr. Davis hit me because I had candy at school."

Mrs. March was angry now.

"Mr. Davis hit you!" she said. "That's not right, and I'm going to write a letter to the school. You can stay at home. Beth's teacher can teach you too."

"Good!" Amy said.

"But Amy," Mrs. March said, "you *were* bad. Mr. Davis doesn't like candy at school, and you know that."

Amy thought about that. Then she said, "Yes, I wasn't very good. I wanted to be important, and that was wrong. I'm sorry."

Amy's mother and her sisters looked at her and smiled.

Chapter 6 Amy is Angry Again

"Meg, Jo, where are you going?" Amy asked one Saturday afternoon.

"You can't come, Amy!" Jo said.

"I know!" Amy said. "You're going to the theater with Laurie. I'm coming, too! I have a little money."

"It isn't for little girls," Jo said. "And Laurie asked *us*."

Amy was very angry.

"You're going to be sorry, Jo March," she said.

Then Laurie arrived, and Meg and Jo went to the theater with him.

◆

In the morning, Jo asked, "Where's my book?"

Jo liked writing stories, and she was a good writer. There was many years' work in that book.

Meg and Beth said, "We don't know."

Amy was quiet.

"Do you have it, Amy?" Jo asked.

"No, I don't," Amy said.

"Amy . . .!" Jo said. "Where is it?"

"I burned it!" Amy answered.

"You burned my book!" said Jo, "My stories were in it! You bad girl!"

She hit Amy and walked away.

Later, Jo came down again.

"I'm very, very sorry, Jo!" Amy said.

But Jo didn't look at her.

In the evening, Mrs. March talked to Jo.

"Amy did a very bad thing," she said. She kissed her daughter. "But please be friends with her. Don't be angry now."

"I don't like her, and I don't want to be friends," Jo answered, and she went to bed.

♦

The morning after that, Jo thought, "I want to be happy today. I'm going to go ice skating with Laurie."

She and Laurie walked down the road with their skates. Amy watched them. She wanted to go too.

Meg said to her, "Go after them. Kiss Jo, and say 'sorry' again."

Amy walked to the river behind Jo and Laurie. Then Jo and Laurie started to skate, and Amy skated too. Jo didn't look at her and Laurie didn't see her.

Then Amy moved away from them. The ice was thin there and suddenly—CRACK! She went down into the cold water.

"Help! Help me!" Amy called.

Jo looked now.

"Oh, no! Amy!" she said. "We're coming, Amy!"

Jo and Laurie quickly helped Amy out of the water. She was very cold. Her face and hands were blue.

They went home quickly, and Hannah went to Amy's bedroom with her.

Later, Jo was in Amy's room with her mother. They talked quietly.

"Is Amy going to get well?" Jo asked.

"Yes," Mrs. March said. "You came home very quickly. You helped her."

Jo said, "I was very angry with Amy, but now I'm sorry. I'm often angry. What can I do?"

She looked at her sister. She was beautiful with her yellow hair. Amy opened her eyes and looked at Jo. They kissed, and they were friends again.

"Jo," said Mother, "you *are* very angry sometimes. You can stop that. Please try! But you're a good girl, and I love you."

Jo kissed her mother.

Chapter 7   Meg's Glove

In the summer, Laurie said to the March girls, "Let's put a letter box in the tree in front of your house. Then I can send you letters."

The girls liked the box. Beth opened it every day.

The girls liked the box.

One day she said, "There's a letter for Miss Amy."

"Thank you," Amy said.

"There are two letters for Miss Jo—and a very old hat!"

"I burn my face every day in this sun," Jo said. "Laurie's a good boy."

"And there's a present for Miss Meg March."

"It's a letter—and my glove," Meg said. "But there's only *one* glove. I had two gloves at the Laurences' house yesterday."

"There was only one glove in the box," Beth said. "Were you with Mr. Brooke yesterday?"

"Yes," Meg said. "He wanted to read a story to me."

Mrs. March looked quickly at her daughter. Meg was very beautiful, but she was a child. Her mother smiled.

◆

That summer was a happy time, but winter came. In October the days were cold and short.

Jo was in the house one day. She looked at the little book in front of her.

"There!" she said. "I can take it now."

She went quietly out of the window. Her mother and sisters didn't see her.

Jo went to an office in town. Laurie was in town too, and he waited for her. She came out into the street, and her face was red.

"What's wrong?" Laurie asked.

"I went to the newspaper office with two stories," Jo said. "The man said, 'Come again in a week.' He's going to read them."

She looked at the little book in front of her.

"That's very good!" Laurie said. "Josephine March, the famous American writer! But Jo, I want to talk to you about Meg's glove—I know about it."

"Where *is* the glove?" Jo asked.

"It's in Mr. Brooke's coat," Laurie said.

"Oh no!" Jo thought. "Mr. Brooke loves Meg! He's going to take her away from us!"

♦

Two weeks later, Jo came into the house with a newspaper.

"Are there any good stories in the newspaper?" Meg asked.

"Yes," Jo answered. "There's one good story."

"Please read it to us," Amy said.

The three sisters listened.

"It's good! Who's the writer?" Beth asked.

"Your sister." Jo smiled.

"You!" Meg said.

"Yes, me!"

"It's *very* good!" Amy said.

"Oh, Jo!" Hannah said.

Mother smiled and kissed her daughter. "Father's going to be very happy."

Chapter 8   Jo's Hair

The letter arrived in early November. Laurie was at the March house with the girls and their mother.

The letter said:

Mrs. March,
Mr. March is in Washington and he is very sick. Please come quickly.
From, S. Hale.

The girls were very unhappy. Mrs. March's face was white.

"Children, listen to me!" she said. "Help me, please. Laurie, please write to Mr. Hale. I'm going to take the morning train."

"Yes, Mrs. March," Laurie said.

"Jo, take a letter to Aunt March. I'm going to ask her for money. Beth, ask Mr. Laurence for food and drink for Mr. March. Amy, get my black bag. Meg, come and help me."

Later, Mr. Brooke came to the house.

He said to Meg, "Miss March, I want to go with your mother tomorrow. I can do some work for Mr. Laurence in Washington too."

"Thank you," Meg said. "Mother would like that."

Mrs. March came in.

"Yes, thank you, Mr. Brooke," she said. Then she asked, "Where's Jo?"

The front door opened. It was Jo.

"Jo—your hair!" Mrs. March said. Jo's hair was very short. "What did you do?"

"Aunt March is reading your letter," she said. "But here's some money for Father from me. I went to a man in town. He buys hair."

"Oh, Jo, thank you," Mrs. March said. "I love you for this."

"Oh, Jo, thank you," Mrs. March said.

Jo smiled at her mother, but that night she didn't sleep.

"What's wrong, Jo?" Meg asked.

"My hair!" Jo said. Her eyes were red. "My hair!"

Chapter 9   Beth is Sick

The girls said goodbye to their mother. Every day they did their work, but they thought about her.

One day, Beth said to Jo and Meg, "Please go and see the Hummels."

"I can't go. Can you go, Jo?" Meg asked.

"No, I have a cold," Jo answered.

"Can you go, Beth?" Meg asked.

"I go every day, because Mother isn't here. But one child is very sick and I can't help her. Please go."

"I can go tomorrow," Meg said.

Beth went to the Hummel's house. Later, she came home. She was very unhappy.

"What's wrong, Beth?" Jo asked.

"Oh, Jo. The child's dead. I stayed with her and Mrs. Hummel went to the doctor's house. He came, but the child was dead. It was scarlet fever. And now I'm sick too."

"Oh no!" Jo said. "I'm going to get Hannah."

Hannah looked at Beth and called Dr. Bangs.

"Amy," Jo said, "you're going to Aunt March's house."

"No!" Amy said.

"Yes," Hannah said. "Do you want scarlet fever?"

◆

Later in the week, Beth was very sick. Jo stayed with her. She washed her sister's face and talked to her. But Beth didn't know Jo, Meg, or Hannah. Jo wanted her mother, but her father was sick too. They didn't write to Mrs. March about Beth.

Dr. Bangs came every day. One day, he looked at Beth and said, "Please write to Mrs. March now."

Then Laurie came to the house.

"Your mother knows about Beth," he said. "Your father isn't very sick now, and she's coming home this evening. I didn't wait—"

"Oh, Laurie!" Jo said. "Thank you!"

In Beth's bedroom, Meg and Jo looked at Beth's face. It was white.

Jo thought, "Oh no, my sister's dead!" She kissed her and said, "Goodbye Beth, goodbye."

But Hannah looked at the child and smiled.

"Beth isn't dead," she said. "She's sleeping! She's going to be well again!"

There was a noise at the door.

"Listen, girls!" Hannah said.

Laurie called, "She's here! Mrs. March is home!"

Chapter 10   What is Love?

Mrs. March came into the room. Meg and Jo kissed her.

Then Beth slowly opened her eyes and smiled.

Mrs. March stayed with her all night. In the morning, Jo went into Beth's room.

"Mother, I want to talk to you," she said. "Mr. Brooke loves Meg. Did you know that? I don't like it."

"I know," Mrs. March said. "John Brooke talked to your father and me in Washington. Does Meg love him too?"

"I don't know," Jo said. "I don't know about love. I liked Mr. Brooke's letters about Father, and I like his eyes. But I want Meg here, at home with us."

"John's a very good man," said Mrs. March. "He helped Father. But don't think about it now. Christmas is coming."

♦

On Christmas Day, Beth was in bed but Amy was home again. It was a good day. There were beautiful presents from Laurie and Mr. Laurence.

Then Laurie arrived.

"And here's a *big* Christmas present for the March family!" he said.

He opened the door again, and there was Mr. March. The girls went to their father and kissed him. They were very, very happy.

"Quietly, girls!" Mrs. March said. "Beth is sleeping!"

But Beth came down from her bedroom.

"Oh, Father, it's you!" she said.

♦

In the morning, Mr. Brooke talked to Meg.

"I love you," he said. "Do you love me?"

"I'm only seventeen," Meg said. "I don't know . . ."

Then Aunt March came into the room. Mr. Brooke went out quickly.

"Where are your mother and father?" Aunt March said. "And what's that man saying to you?"

"He's father's friend, Aunt March!" Meg said.

"Then why is your face red?" Aunt March said. "You can't marry *him*. He doesn't have any money! I'm not going to give you *my* money."

Meg was very angry.

"I don't want your money, Aunt March! John loves me, and he's a good man. We can work for our money. I *am* going to marry him."

"Marry him, then! I don't want to see you again!"

Aunt March walked out of the house.

Meg didn't move. She looked out the window at her aunt's back.

Mr. Brooke came into the room again.

"My love—I listened. Thank you, thank you," he said. "Can I ask you again . . .?"

Meg looked into his eyes.

"Oh, John, the answer's *yes*. I'm going to marry you—and we're going to be very happy."

◆

Later, Jo talked to Laurie.

"I love Meg, and I want her with me," she said. "But she's going to be happy, and that's good. And *I'm* happy today. Mother and Father are here. Beth is well again. Meg loves John. Amy and I are friends—and you and I are friends too. I'm writing, and people like my stories. But Laurie, are we going to be happy in a year, or in two years? Who knows?"

ACTIVITIES

Chapters 1–5

Before you read

1 Read the introduction to the book.
   a When did Louisa May Alcott write this story?
   b Does the story start in summer or in winter?
   c Who is the story about?
   d Which country are they in?

2 Find the words in *italics* in your dictionary. They are in the story. Answer the questions.
   a Do you like:
      acting?
      candy?
      parties?
      presents?
   b Is your *aunt* your mother's brother?
   c Your book is *burning*. Is it hot or cold?
   d Do you:
      curl your hair?
      play the *piano*?
      put *ribbons* in your hair?
      have *gloves*?
   e Who
      helps with your homework?
      do you *kiss*?
   f Was there a *war* in your country? When? Why?

3 Are these sentences about yesterday, often, or now?
   a I'm thinking about my family.   c My brother hits me.
   b I *thought* about my family.   d My brother *hit* me.

26

After you read

4 Answer the questions.

    a What are the names of the March sisters?

    b Where is Mr. March?

    c Who eats the Marches' food on Christmas morning?

    d Who is Laurie?

    e Why does Mr. Davis hit Amy?

5 Who says these sentences?

    a "It's Christmas, girls. Can we give them our food?"

    b "My hair! My hair! I can't go to the party now!"

    c "I *was* sick, but now I'm well again."

    d "I wanted to be important, and that was wrong."

Chapters 6–10

Before you read

6 Look at the pictures in the book. Who can you see? What are they doing?

7 Look at these words. Put them in the sentences.

    box (n)   *ice marry scarlet fever skate*

    a ..... is very cold.

    b He's sick. He has ..... .

    c Put the books in a ..... !

    d We ..... on the river in winter.

    e She's going to ..... my brother.

After you read

8 Answer the questions.

    a Why does Amy burn Jo's book?

    b What does Meg get from the letter box?

    c How does Jo get money for her father?

    d Why is Beth sick?

    e When does Mr. March come home?

9 Work with a friend.

Student A: You are Meg. You are going to marry John Brooke. Talk to Jo about it.

Student B: You are Jo. Meg is your friend. You want her at home with you. Talk to her about it.

Writing

10 Which sister do you like? Why? Write about her.

11 There are four books about the March family. Did you like this book? What are the sisters going to do in the three books after this? What do you think?